RACIAL LITERACY

Navigating Intersectionality

How Race, Class, and Gender Overlap

Jamila Osman

E **Enslow Publishing**
101 W. 23rd Street
Suite 240
New York, NY 10011
USA

enslow.com

Published in 2019 by Enslow Publishing, LLC.
101 W. 23rd Street, Suite 240, New York, NY 10011

Library of Congress Cataloging-in-Publication Data

Names: Osman, Jamila, author.
Title: Navigating intersectionality : how race, class, and gender overlap / Jamila
  Osman.
Description: New York, NY : Enslow Publishing, [2019] | Series: Racial literacy |
  Audience: Grade 7–12. | Includes bibliographical references and index.
Identifiers: LCCN 2018020654| ISBN 9781978504653 (library bound) | ISBN
  9781978505605 (pbk.)
Subjects: LCSH: Intersectionality (Sociology) | Group identity.
Classification: LCC HM488.5 .O86 2019 | DDC 305—dc23
LC record available at https://lccn.loc.gov/2018020654

Printed in the United States of America

To Our Readers: We have done our best to make sure all website addresses in this book were active and appropriate when we went to press. However, the author and the publisher have no control over and assume no liability for the material available on those websites or on any websites they may link to. Any comments or suggestions can be sent by email to customerservice@enslow.com.

Photo Credits: Cover, p. 1 aberCPC/Alamy Stock Photo; p. 5 Joseph Sohm/ Shutterstock.com; pp. 6–7 Dick Swanson/The LIFE Images Collection/Getty Images; p. 9 Iamnee/Shutterstock.com; p. 11 Amanda Edwards/Getty Images; p. 14 Jack Mitchell/Archive Photos/Getty Images; p. 17 Florilegius/SSPL/Getty Images; pp. 18–19 Lambert/Hulton Fine Art Collection/Getty Images; p. 23 Private Collection /Bridgeman Images; pp. 25, 26, 60–61, 68 © AP Images; pp. 28–29 Bryan R. Smith/ AFP/Getty Images; pp. 31, 42 Bettmann/Getty Images; pp. 32–33 Private Collection /Wood Ronsaville Harlin, Inc. USA/Bridgeman Images; p. 35 Hulton Archive/Getty Images; p. 37 Archive Holdings Inc./Archive Photos/Getty Images; p. 39 The Washington Post/Getty Images; p. 44 Treible/MCT/Newscom; p. 48 Pacific Press/ LightRocket/Getty Images; p. 50 Robyn Beck/AFP/Getty Images; pp. 52–53 Mark Reinstein/Corbis News/Getty Images; pp. 56–57 Chip Somodevilla/Getty Images; p. 63 Nicolas McComber/E+/Getty Images; pp. 64–65 Steve Debenport E+/ Getty Images; p. 66 Ethel Wolvovitz/Alamy Stock Photo; cover and interior pages background design Ensuper/Shutterstock.com (colors), Miloje/Shutterstock.com (texture).

CONTENTS

Introduction

Over the last few years, the emergence of the Black Lives Matter and #MeToo movements has forced race and gender to become an integral part of the national conversation—regardless of whether or not people felt ready to have these particular conversations. For far too long, talking about race, class, and gender was taboo. But events of the last few years, from the election of Donald Trump as president, to the rise in hate crimes against minorities, to increased xenophobia and anti-immigrant rhetoric, have required an examination and discussion of power and identity in society. While these are conversations many people feel ill-equipped to have, we must insist on having them. This is not a conversation anyone should get to opt out of, especially not young people who are going to shape the future of this country and the world.

A woman holds a Black Lives Matter sign at a MLK Jr. Day event in Los Angeles.

Thousands of demonstrators gather around the Washington Monument protesting the Vietnam War.

Young people have historically been at the forefront of social movements in the United States and across the world. We can see this today in the way young people take on leadership in Black Lives Matter or organize demonstrations against gun violence. In history classes, a mantra we hear again and again is that those who do not learn from the past are doomed to repeat it. The United States is a country with a rich history of social movements. These movements have much to teach us as a new generation rises to the challenge of creating a more fair and equitable society. We can and must learn from the mistakes and failures that different groups struggling to gain equality have made in the past. As we celebrate the length we've come, we must never lose sight of all the work that we still have to do.

CHAPTER 1

Identity and Intersectionality

What do we mean when we talk about *identity*? It is a word that is used quite often in many different contexts, and yet it is hard to define. Different people mean different things when they use that term. A psychologist's definition of the word is not the same as a sociologist's. Ultimately, when discussing identity, we are referring to who we are and how the world sees us. Our identities are the multiple characteristics, both visible and invisible, that identify us as individuals and members of a group.

Who Are You?

Ernest Hemingway, the American novelist, developed the Iceberg Theory of Literature,[1] which can be applied to better understand the concept of identity. Roughly one-eighth of an iceberg is visible to the human eye from the surface of the water. The majority of the iceberg is submerged below water. Likewise, we often meet people, see the visible markers of their identity, and assume we know who they are. While there are certainly some visible signs of identity, the vast majority of identity markers exist below the surface. Some visible identity characteristics include, but are not limited to, someone's race, gender, age,

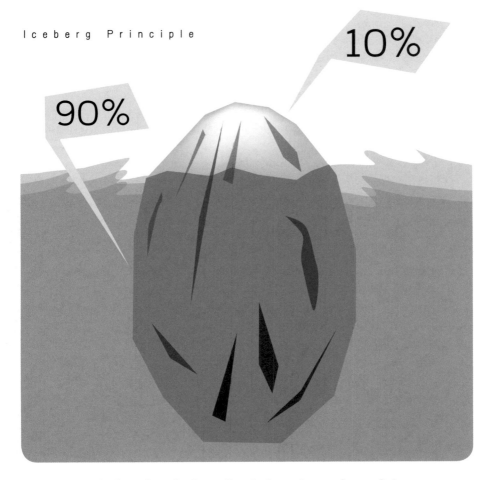

Iceberg Principle

10%

90%

The majority of an iceberg lies below the surface of the water.

physical appearance, physical ability, and dress. While these aspects of one's identity are important, we can't assume this is someone's entire story. There is a lot we cannot tell about someone just by looking at them. Some of the identity markers that exist below the surface include, but are not limited to, ethnicity, nationality, documentation status, sexual orientation, beliefs, and values.

Our identities shape our experiences and worldview. They are extremely important in understanding our individual and collective relationships to power and privilege in society. Some identities are less oppressed than others, while others experience more oppression. The three most useful markers in understanding one's subject position in society are race, class, and gender. The ways in which these identities are interconnected is called intersectionality. Intersectionality refers to the idea that social categorizations like race, class, and gender create interconnected systems of oppression and discrimination. While this term has skyrocketed in usage and popularity over the last few years, it is far from a new concept.

The Mother of Intersectionality

Born in 1959 in Canton, Ohio, Kimberlé Williams Crenshaw is heralded for coining the term "intersectionality" in her seminal paper "Mapping the Margins: Intersectionality, Identity Politics, and Violence Against Women of Color."[2] The term quickly became part of mainstream feminist vocabulary. A civil rights attorney and critical race theorist, Crenshaw felt she needed a term to address the ways in which race and

Kimberlé Crenshaw delivers a rousing speech at the 2018 Women's March in Los Angeles.

gender overlap to explain the experiences of women of color in the legal system.

Her desire to look at the world from an intersectional lens began during her years as a college student. She noticed that while she could take courses on race and courses on gender, there were none that explored the intersection of both. As a law student at Harvard Law School, she began raising questions about the nature of anti-discrimination laws in the United States. Anti-discrimination laws looked at gender and race as separate issues, and as a result Black women and other women of color, who face overlapping forms of discrimination on the basis of both their gender and race, were left at a disadvantage.

When asked about inspiration for the term, Crenshaw often cites the legal case *Degraffenreid v. General Motors*, a case in which five Black women attempted to sue General Motors for racial and gender discrimination. Throughout the trial, the women and their lawyers had to clearly demonstrate that the discrimination they were facing was the result of two different kinds of policies. In an interview on intersectionality with *New Statesman* in 2014, Crenshaw said:

> "The particular challenge in the law was one that was grounded in the fact that anti-discrimination law looks at race and gender separately... The consequence of that is when African American women or any other women of colour experience either compound or overlapping discrimination, the law initially just was not there to come to their defence."[3]

Though grounded in her work as a legal scholar, her theory gave a new generation of feminists and activists a new lens through which to understand the complexity of identity as it related to various overlapping vectors of oppression.

Existing at the Intersection

Kimberlé Crenshaw's work was built on the legacy of Black feminist activists and theorists who had long explored the intersections of race, class, and gender in their work. Audre Lorde, feminist scholar and poet, once said, "There is no such thing as a single-issue struggle because we do not live single-issue lives."[4]

This quote clearly illuminates the theory of intersectionality as it relates to understanding the human condition and our movements for social justice. To look at race, class, and gender as separate spheres is to ignore the ways these social categories intersect and complicate our relationship to power in society. It was the hope of not just Crenshaw, but the women theorists who came before her, that we would one day live in a world where power was not concentrated in the hands of a few, but equally distributed among the masses of people.

It was long believed that there was a hierarchy of oppression: that identity was a ladder, and those at the top of the ladder were closest to the center of power and those at the bottom were furthest away. This imagery means those

Audre Lorde and Intersectional Identity

Audre Lorde was a widely acclaimed poet, novelist, feminist scholar, and activist who was born on February 18, 1934, in New York City to immigrant parents from the island of Granada. Identity was a huge theme in many of her works. She wrote extensively about how her identity as a "black, lesbian, mother, warrior, poet"[5] shaped the way she saw the world. She used her influence as a poet to address issues of social injustice and inequality. One of her most famous works is *The Cancer Journals,* which chronicles her battle with breast cancer, a battle she ultimately lost in 1992.[6]

Feminist scholar and acclaimed poet Audre Lorde (1992)

at the bottom of the ladder must trample over everyone else in order to replace those at the top. Audre Lorde, who described herself as a Black lesbian, feminist, socialist, said there is no hierarchy of oppression,[7] and it does no good to look at various forms of oppression as separate from each other, but interconnected. We will achieve justice only when we are able to build a mass movement that addresses every segment of society and accounts for all the needs of the oppressed people of the world.

In the next chapters, we will define race, class, and gender as separate but interconnected social categories. We will look at the ways past social movements have shaped the development of intersectionality and how this theory is shaping many of the social movements of today.

CHAPTER 2

Understanding Race

In recent years, race and racism have been at the forefront of conversations in the United States. One cannot study the history of the United States without learning about the history of racism that is deeply engrained in this country. The Student Nonviolent Coordinating Committee, Brown Berets, Yellow Peril, Black Panthers, and most recently, Black Lives Matter are all examples of activist groups who have challenged racism in this country and actively worked to improve the lives and material reality of people of color in the United States. It seems as though most people have decided that racism in the United States is just a fact of life and there is no way to completely eradicate it. But racism has not always been a fact of life, and it is important to trace the origins of racism and race-based classifications to the formation of the United States.

A Brief History of Race

It is true that human beings have always noticed the ways in which they were different from others and grouped themselves based on these differences. For much of the world's history, human beings were categorized by their religious beliefs, language and cultural background, social status, or class affiliation. It was uncommon for human beings to categorize themselves based on race and other physical differences. In the United States, the division of people by race and the institutionalization of racism began with the

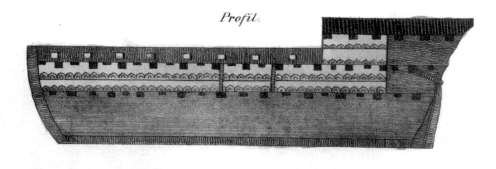

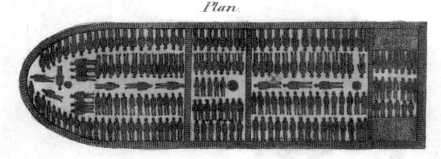

An illustration of a ship shows hundreds of enslaved Africans on the lower deck.

transatlantic slave trade. The emergence of race as a way of categorizing people and then ascribing positive or negative attributes to them also did not begin until the transatlantic slave trade. European settlers did not invent slavery— people had been enslaved in various cultures and contexts since the beginning of history. But the fact that slavery in the United States was determined solely by race was what made it a particularly unique phenomenon. For the first time in history, race became the rationalization for enslaving other people.

In order to fully understand the development of racism in the United States, we have to go back to early colonial America and examine the contradictions that laid the foundation of this country. In traditional history books, the fight for independence from Great Britain is seen as noble and courageous. Europeans fled the oppression of their monarch King George to begin their own country—a country that would be rooted in the freedom and justice they could not find in Europe. What is missing from this story is the oppression that European settlers committed against the Indigenous population of what was then called Turtle Island. The settlers did not "found" a country—one cannot discover a land that already was inhabited by many thriving Indigenous cultures and communities. From its inception, freedom and

A painting by W. J. Aylward depicts the arrival of the pilgrims at Plymouth Rock.

justice did not include the Indigenous peoples of the United States. Freedom and justice was obtained for European settlers at their expense. This was the foremost contradiction of this so-called New World.

Stolen Africans were not the first slaves in the United States. Colonists tried to enslave white indentured servants, primarily Irish, who had debts to pay off. This was not a viable economic model because when they paid off their debts, they would be free. Irish indentured servants were often indistinguishable from free Europeans. When they escaped, which was often, it was impossible to find them. The settlers also tried to enslave Native Americans, but were unsuccessful. Because Indigenous people knew the land, they were often good at evading capture and escaping if caught.

Africans and white indentured servants worked side by side during this time. They often intermarried and raised children together. Working conditions were abusive and intolerable. The tension of poor working conditions and abuse came to a head during what would come to be called Bacon's Rebellion, when white indentured servants and enslaved Africans joined forces to attack the slave owners and bosses.[1] This terrified the political and class elites who saw this alliance as a threat to their power. As a result, they decided the system of indentured servitude was too unreliable. This posed a significant dilemma in the minds of the early settlers. The economy of the United States was almost exclusively dependent on slave labor. They needed a permanent and inexhaustible labor source. As more and

Maroon Colonies and Early Resistance

During the colonial era, many Africans escaped slavery and banded together to form what came to be called maroon colonies. Maroon colonies were usually established in places with harsh geographic landscapes, such as swamps and mountainous areas. The harsh terrain was a deterrent from European settlers who could capture fugitive slaves. Many fugitive slaves mixed with the Indigenous peoples of the Americas and formed their own autonomous communities. This was one of the many ways that enslaved Africans resisted the brutality of slavery.

more indentured servants worked off their debts, colonists turned to Africans for more and more labor.

This presented colonists with another contradiction they would have to struggle to solve. How could a country founded on ideals of freedom and democracy enslave an entire population? How could they claim to be a land for the free while justifying what was quickly becoming the most abusive and horrific slave trade history had ever seen? Race was the answer to that question. If Africans were property and *not* people, if racism could somehow be codified into law, and Africans could be positioned at the very bottom of the social hierarchy based purely on race, then slavery could be justified. This is what the colonists set out to do, and the advent of racism in the modern world is evidence of their success. For the first time in human history, racism had become codified into law, and race-based distinctions among people were seen as natural and innate.

No Progress Without Struggle: The Abolition Movement

One of the first large-scale, race-based movements in the United States was the abolitionist movement. As the evils of slavery became clearer, the abolitionist movement began to gain traction. Made up of European settlers and currently and formerly enslaved Africans, the movement sought to end the evils of slavery in the United States once and for all. As the abolitionist movement was gaining traction and support, the early wave of the feminist movement was developing. Unfortunately, both of these movements were seen as competing against one another. Abolitionists were afraid to address what was referred to as the "Woman's Question."[2] They were worried it would turn men who would otherwise support the abolition of slavery away from the cause. This erased the experiences of Black women, who suffered doubly under the brutal institution of slavery. African men and women had a shared history of race-based abuse at the hands of slave owners, but women faced additional horrors because of their status as women. Because slaves were seen as the property of their owners, this included even their bodies, and for women this meant they were constantly victims of sexual abuse and rape at the hands of their owners.

Intersectionality means racism cannot be seen within the context of skin color alone. It accounts for the myriad ways people experience oppression under an abusive system. Intersectionality begs us to ask the question: What would it mean to end the system of slavery, if Black women (along with other women) were still seen as the property of men?

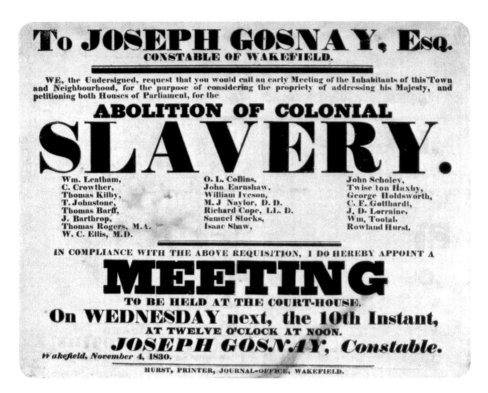

A flyer calling a meeting to discuss the abolition of slavery

All Power to the People: Intersectionality in the Black Panther Party

It seems the history of the United States is a history of oppression and the struggle against it. In the 1960s, the Civil Rights Movement exploded and would forever change the trajectory and the conversation surrounding race relations in the United States.

It is virtually impossible to study the Civil Rights Movement without coming across mention of the Black

Panther Party. Whether they are glorified by supporters or vilified by racists, the images used to depict them are the same. Images of Huey P. Newton and Stokely Carmichael are featured in textbooks. All of these photographic and written depictions of the party have one thing in common—they are image after image of male party members. If one was to base their understanding of the Panthers on these images, they would think women had little to no involvement in the party. This couldn't be further from the truth. Women in the Black Panther Party were essential to the organization. It is sexism that erases their contributions and glorifies the contributions of men in the party.

Intersectionality asks us to ask questions of history. It asks us to question the experiences of women in the Black Panther Party. In what ways did their gender identity shape their experiences in the party and their analysis of racism in the '60s?

Women in the Black Panther Party were vocal critics of racial oppression in the United States. But they were doubly exploited on the basis of their gender and race in ways that Black men were not. Not only were they forced to struggle against racism with Black male allies, they also had to struggle against the sexism they consistently faced.

Elaine Brown, a Black Panther Party member and one of its female leaders, was an outspoken critic of sexism not just in the United States, but in the party in particular. In her 1992 memoir *A Taste of Power*, she describes the ways she organized alongside other women to challenge the patriarchal tendencies of men within the party. She made

Armed Black Panther Party members Bobby Seale and Huey Newton stand in front of their Oakland office.

Elaine Brown stands outside a museum in Oakland, California, on the fiftieth anniversary of the Black Panther Party.

the link between racial and gender oppression clear and inextricable from one another when she said she came to the conclusion that, "Racism and sexism in America were equal partners in [her] oppression."[3]

CHAPTER 3

Understanding Gender

For much of US history, feminism has cycled in and out of popularity. Each wave of feminism, from first wave to third, has had different goals and aspirations. Early in the feminist movement's history, it failed to look at gender and the experiences of women through an intersectional lens. Because of this failure, it often alienated women of color, poor women, and transgender women. A popular definition of feminism throughout much of feminist history is "the radical notion that women are people."[1] Throughout US history, women were seen as the property of their fathers and then the men they married. The women's movement sought to change the conditions of women by first getting women the right to vote, the right to divorce abusive husbands, the right to own property, and the right to work and receive equal compensation for their labor. While all women face sexist oppression in a patriarchal society, these experiences vary in

Women's Rights are Human Rights

Coinciding with the election of Donald Trump as president, the Women's March became one of the largest demonstrations in US history. Organized by an intersectional group of women, the march hoped to channel the political power of all women to transform society for the better. Marching under the slogan "Women's Rights Are Human Rights, and Human Rights Are Women's Rights,"[2] the organizers recognized that though they shared womanhood, their experiences were drastically different depending on other identities. Although the focal march happened in Washington, DC, there were similar protests in almost every state in the country. This became one of the largest single-day demonstrations in US history.

Thousands of protestors march through the streets of New York City during the 2017 Women's March.

severity depending on a woman's race, class, and sexuality. The early iterations of the feminist movement failed to acknowledge these differences in women's experiences.

The Suffragettes and the Fight for the Right to Vote

At the height of the abolition movement in the United States, when people worked together to end the institution of slavery, the women's movement began to take off. Women, primarily white women, began to look at the abusive conditions of their own lives and realized that though their chains were different than those that bound enslaved Africans, they were not free either.

One of the first demands that women made during the first wave of the feminist movement was the right to vote. They wanted to add a federal amendment that would grant women this right. One cannot examine first wave feminism and the battle for suffrage without examining the contradictions that activists at the time were confronted with.

The early suffragettes fell into two camps. Some of them were abolitionists who felt that the struggle for Black liberation from slavery had to go hand-in-hand with the struggle for women's rights. There were also those who felt that women's rights had to be secured first as it would be an easier struggle to win, and focusing on race would distract from gains that were to be made. Many of the earliest suffragettes, those whose names are most well-known and lauded in textbooks, like Susan B. Anthony and Elizabeth

Members of the Woman Suffrage Party pose with the US flag.

Cady Stanton, were openly hostile to the needs of Black women in the movement.[3]

There was a great deal of crossover between the abolitionist movement and the women's rights movement. Frederick Douglass, a formerly enslaved Black man and one of the key leaders in the fight to end slavery, was a staunch supporter of women's rights. Some of the leading women in the early women's movement first began their activism in anti-slavery work. It was in many of these anti-slavery organizations and meetings that women like sisters Angelina and Sarah Grimké learned that many of the men who wanted to end slavery did not care about the oppression of women, would ignore their contributions, and deny them leadership opportunities in the movement.[4] The 1848 Seneca Falls Convention, the first women's rights convention organized in the United States, brought together the most active voices in the struggle for both women's rights and abolition, bringing to light the complicated ways in which both movements needed to coexist in order to succeed.[5]

Ain't I a Woman?

While the early women's rights movement tended to ignore Black women and the issues that applied specifically to them,

Elizabeth Cady Stanton gives a speech at the 1848 Seneca Falls Convention.

some made their voices heard. Sojourner Truth delivered her famous "Ain't I a Woman?" speech exploring the connection between race and gender in 1851.[6] Truth was active in the abolitionist movement and the women's rights movement. Born into slavery, she escaped with her daughter to freedom in 1827. She spent the entirety of her life organizing against the oppression she faced as a Black woman.

In 1851, she was a speaker at the Ohio Women's Rights Convention. In an impassioned and impromptu speech, she spoke at length about the erasure of the experiences of Black women from the discourse surrounding the women's rights movement. She said she was concerned that if the abolition movement were successful, it would be at the expense of *both* Black and white women who would be left disenfranchised (without the right to vote) and without any of the political protections or rights of men. She clearly articulated the ways in which the experiences of white women and Black women were different:

> "That man over there says that women need to be helped into carriages, and lifted over ditches, and to have the best place everywhere. Nobody ever helps me into carriages, or over mud-puddles, or gives me any best place! And ain't I a woman? Look at me! Look at my arm! I have ploughed and planted, and gathered into barns, and no man could head me! And ain't I a woman? I could work as much and eat as much as a man - when I could get it - and bear the lash as well! And ain't I a woman? I have borne thirteen children, and seen most all sold off to slavery, and when I cried out with my mother's grief, none but Jesus heard me! And ain't I a woman?"[7]

Portrait of civil rights leader Sojourner Truth (1797–1883)

Sojourner Truth was not the only Black woman to speak out against the invisibility of Black women in the early feminist movement. As the aims and aspirations of the feminist movement expanded and changed in the following years, the call for intersectionality would be raised time and again.

Working Women

After the Nineteenth Amendment granted women the right to vote, the feminist movement began to take on other aspects of women's oppression. The second wave of feminism started to gain traction around the same time as the peak of the Civil Rights Movement in the United States. This second wave was concerned with the rights of women to work and exist outside of their homes. Feminist thinkers of this era were concerned with creating a notion of women's work that existed beyond housework and childrearing. This wave of the feminist movement was also concerned with women's reproductive rights and pushed for access to abortion. These concerns were primarily being raised by white women, and with the previous wave of feminism, poor, lesbian, transgender, and women of color pushed for more expansive demands and a more intersectional lens to understand the status and experiences of all women.

One of the key demands of the feminist movement was the right for women to work outside of the home. Unlike many of the middle-class white women who pushed for this, poor women and women of color had *always* worked outside the home out of necessity. They needed to work in order to

Unlike women of color, white women often didn't need to work outside the home for their family's survival. They felt trapped in their houses, while the women of color's labor was often exploited both in and outside the home.

care for and sustain their families. For them, work was not a luxury or a privilege, but another form of exploitation that kept them away from their families and children. It was poor women and women of color who cleaned the homes of middle-class white women.

Betty Friedan wrote *The Feminine Mystique*, a book that was lauded as a central text in the development and understanding of second wave feminism.[8] In this book,

Friedan explored the unhappiness women felt since they were often isolated in their homes bound to housework and childrearing. She called this housewife's syndrome.[9] Friedan, a middle-class and well-educated white woman, failed to acknowledge that this was a uniquely white middle-class experience. She didn't address the fact that when white women got the jobs they so desperately sought, poor women and women of color would be the ones to raise their children at the expense of their own. The white middle-class woman's experience was universalized as the default experience of all women and failed to look intersectionally at the myriad experiences of women under patriarchy. Women who were marginalized in other ways continued to push for intersectionality during the second wave of feminism as they challenged this archetype of womanhood, and worked to reinterpret feminism on their own terms.

bell hooks and the Borders Between Women

bell hooks is one of the most prominent feminist thinkers of the second wave feminist movement. Her seminal text *Ain't I a Woman: Black Feminism and Women* was a nod to Sojourner Truth's 1851 speech. In this book, hooks (born Gloria Jean Watkins) clearly illustrated the ways in which multiple social classifications were interconnected. She was an early critic of the exclusionary tendencies of the second wave feminism and pushed for a more expansive understanding of what it means to be a woman. In her book, she wrote about the importance of a sisterhood that transcended the arbitrary borders of race that divided women from one another. She wrote:

> "Women, all women, are accountable for racism continuing to divide us. Our willingness to assume responsibility for the elimination of racism need not be engendered by feelings of guilt, moral responsibility, victimization, or rage. It can spring from a heartfelt desire for sisterhood and the personal, intellectual realization that racism among women undermines the potential radicalism of feminism. It can spring from our knowledge that racism is an obstacle in our path that must be removed."[10]

Feminist scholar bell hooks during an interview in 1999

She believed that racism within the women's movement would stifle the movement for social justice as a whole, and as long as this racism existed, the women's movement would never succeed. As bell hooks and other women of color became more and more vocal about the urgency of intersectionality in the feminist movement, they shifted the trajectory and aims of the movement and changed the public understanding of what it meant and looked like to be a woman.

CHAPTER 4

Understanding Class

People have attempted to understand the relationship people have to wealth and money for many centuries. Karl Marx, a German philosopher, economist, and historian who lived at the turn of the 19th century, developed a theory of understanding how class operates in society. To understand Marxist theory, one has to understand capitalism.

Capitalism is an economic system in which trade and industry are owned and controlled by private owners, rather than by the state, for the purpose of making a profit. Marxist theory states that capitalism is inherently unfair because it is a system of exploitation. Marx said that people are organized into two main groups: the working class, which he called the proletariat, and the ruling class, which he called the bourgeoisie. The working class are the people who work in factories, offices, or farms. The bourgeoisie are the ones who own the factories, land, and farms that the proletariat work in. In Marxist theory,

Karl Marx opened up important social and cultural discussions surrounding class, labor, and economic exploitation.

the ruling class lives off of the exploited labor of workers. He believed that the trajectory of human history was defined by the struggle between the ruling class and the working class because they have competing interests.

These competing interests became most clear in 2011 with the emergence of Occupy Wall Street, a social movement that forced people to begin having honest conversations about social class in the United States—a touchy and often taboo subject.[1] The movement was focused on addressing a central question: Why is it that as the rich get richer, the poor get poorer?

The Haves and Have-Nots: Class Structure in the United States

In the United States, social class is a complicated thing. It is not just the amount of money someone has, although that is certainly part of it. There are typically three tiers that are relevant when defining social class: the upper class, middle class, and lower class. There is a great deal of disparity between these classes, with the richest 1 percent of Americans owning 40 percent of the country's wealth.[2] The fundamental difference between the social classes is the kind of work they do and how that work is perceived. Class correlates to one's educational attainment, occupation, and social networks. It also corresponds to one's political power and voice in society. Each class has its own social norms and values, which make moving between classes a difficult feat to accomplish. Examining class in the United States reveals a lot about the way power and privilege work in society.

Not much trickling down

The richest Americans saw their incomes spike in the past three decades while middle- and low-income earners have had more modest gains.

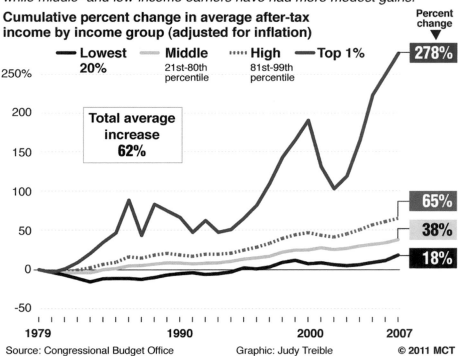

Cumulative percent change in average after-tax income by income group (adjusted for inflation)

Source: Congressional Budget Office   Graphic: Judy Treible   © 2011 MCT

This chart compares the massive spike in the incomes of the richest Americans and the marginal gains made by the middle and lower class.

Those in the upper classes have the most power, while those in the lower classes have significantly less power. The United States is extremely economically stratified—this means there is an unequal and unfair distribution of resources between the classes.

In the United States, the upper class is the highest tier in society. The upper class is the smallest class in the United States. Typically, it has inherited wealth, or wealth that is passed from generation to generation. There is a connection between social class and land ownership, and in the United States the one hundred wealthiest families own as much land as that of New England.[3] In recent years, the income levels of the top tier have continued to grow. The upper class has a larger income and is able to save more money than people in lower classes who have less disposable income. Jobs that are typically considered upper class are physicians, managerial positions, chief executives, lawyers, and other financial specialists.

The middle class in the United States is a social class that is always in flux. There are many who debate whether the middle class even exists anymore. The easiest way to see the middle class is as one that acts as a buffer between the upper class and the lower class. What many economists can agree on, however, is that the middle class has been steadily shrinking over the last decade.[4] The decline of the middle class is a reflection of greater income inequality across the country.

The lower class is not only the class with the least wealth, but the class with the lowest perceived social status. The lower class can be broken down into two groups, according

Redistributing Political and Economic Power

In 1967, Dr. Martin Luther King Jr. had begun to address economic issues just as frequently as he addressed racial issues. He had a radical plan to organize a new March on Washington that would bring together poor people from all across the nation to address income inequality, job security, housing, and education. This was to be called the Poor People's Campaign of 1968. The campaign sought a redistribution of political and economic power in the country from the hands of the elite few to the masses of poor and downtrodden citizens. Many believed the campaign could change the political and economic landscape of the country, but Dr. King was assassinated before it could fully take off.

to sociologist W. Lloyd Warner: the working poor and the underclass.[5] Overall, the term refers to those in low-wage, high-risk jobs that offer little economic compensation or status. Based on 2016 US Census Bureau data, 14 percent of the population lives below the poverty line.[6] This number is estimated to grow in the coming years.

Examining these three classes, it becomes clear that one's social class determines where they fall in the hierarchy of America. The rich and poor are not only divided by enormous sums of wealth, but by other disparities as well. The United States, one of the wealthiest nations in the world, has one of the world's worst health divides between the haves and have-nots. The experiences of people in these different classes, however, are not universal. People are not identified by their socioeconomic status alone: one's class relationship is also affected by their race, gender, and other identities.

Occupy Wall Street: Whose Streets? Our Streets!

In 2011, Occupy Wall Street (OWS), a leaderless movement, took the United States by storm. OWS championed itself as a movement of the 99 percent, "the broad masses of people robbed of their due share of society's wealth and opportunities by millionaires and billionaires."[7] At a time of increasing national and global inequality, OWS began in New York's Zuccotti Park to challenge the increased disparities between the haves and the have-nots. It was the first time in recent history that people aligned on class-based interests. It's most famous slogan, "We Are the 99%,"[8] appealed to a wide swath of Americans who felt disenfranchised or ignored by a government that protected banks and profit over everyday people. It appealed to people who saw similar class interests as a way to bring people together, but addressing class without looking at it through an intersectional lens drove people apart. Angela Davis, a civil rights activist and associate of the Black Panther Party, was a huge supporter of the Occupy movement. Even as she supported the movement, she pushed its organizers to think about how to unite along lines of difference. In an article written for the *Guardian*, she wrote:

> "Occupy activists are thinking deeply about how we might incorporate opposition to racism, class exploitation, homophobia, xenophobia, ableism, violence done to the environment and transphobia into the resistance of the 99% ...

Protesters gather in Zuccotti Park during the 4th anniversary of the Occupy Wall Street protests.

Thus, the most pressing question facing the Occupy activists is how to craft a unity that respects and celebrates the immense differences among the 99%. How can we learn how to come together?"[9]

Intersectionality asks the same question that Angela Davis poses above. How can we, despite our differences, come together? Occupy Wall Street, unfortunately, never figured out how to address these differences effectively and the movement lost support.

CHAPTER 5

Many Struggles, One Movement

Despite Occupy Wall Street's failure to be a truly intersectional movement, there are many historical and contemporary examples of intersectional organizing that we can learn from. History has shown us that when groups are able to organize along multiple lines of identity, they are able to create truly inclusive and transformational movements that are capable of changing society.

Although we all experience the world differently, it is critical that we realize our oppressions, different as they may be, stem from the same root causes and the same flawed system. Though the term "intersectionality" may be relatively new to the public's vocabulary, for as long as people have been demanding systemic change, many people have understood the importance of intersectionality. Throughout history, there have been people who looked at their differences in identity not as points of division, but as points of solidarity. The systems that maintain identity-based oppression are the same systems, and the only way to change them is by working together. From the height of the transatlantic slave trade when Indigenous people fought alongside Africans to fight settlers, to the recent Dakota Access Pipeline protests where people of all races, social classes, and gender identities came together under a single banner, it is clear that the only way to create a world where everyone is treated with dignity and respect is to work collectively.

Native Americans march toward the site of the Dakota Access Pipeline protest and encampment.

Who Wins in a Game of Oppression Olympics?

Have you ever been in a situation where people were comparing oppressions? Person A says, "It's so hard being (INSERT OPPRESSED GROUP HERE), and Person B will scoff and respond, "Oh yeah? Imagine being (INSERT NAME OF OTHER OPPRESSED GROUP HERE)."

Unfortunately, this scenario happens far too frequently when people begin discussions on identity and oppression. This is called Oppression Olympics and describes the competition that occurs when different marginalized groups try and one-up each other to win the title of Most Oppressed.[1] What people often fail to recognize is no one wins in this game. It is possible for multiple groups to be oppressed at the same time. Just because one form of oppression looks different from another doesn't mean it is less important to address it. When people begin playing Oppression Olympics, they get stuck in a never-ending cycle of competition where people's experiences and lived realities are invalidated. As mentioned in chapter 1, Audre Lorde, the feminist scholar and thinker, said there is no hierarchy of oppression.[2] What this shows us is oppression does not look like a ladder. Our identities are not rungs, and no social group needs to be stepped on in order for others to get to the top.

The Rainbow Coalition and Building a United Front

As long as there have been oppressed groups in the United States, there have been groups of people working together along various lines of identity. During the 1960s, at the peak of the Civil Rights Movement, a plethora of groups organized themselves to collectively challenge systems of oppression. It was an alliance between the Chicago chapter of the Black Panthers, the Puerto Rican Young Lords, and a group of poor rural whites who called themselves the Young Patriots. This alliance was known as the Rainbow Coalition.[3] It was a historic moment where people came together across racial and class lines to build power and change what was an intolerable status quo.

The Chicago chapter of the Black Panther Party was led by Fred Hampton, who spearheaded the formation of the Rainbow Coalition. He was active in many Black Panther Party programs, including political education classes, free health clinics, and free breakfast program. He was an invaluable leader of the movement until he was assassinated on December 4, 1969. He was killed in a raid organized by the office of Cook County State Attorney's office in conjunction with the Chicago Police Department and Federal Bureau of Investigation (FBI).[4]

Jack Gordon, Mel Forbes, and Spike Lee gather at the National Rainbow Coalition conference in 1994.

The Young Lords was an organization of Puerto Ricans who wanted to address the racism and discrimination they experienced in the United States. They wanted issues specific to Puerto Ricans to be addressed in the civil rights dialogues of the time. They also campaigned extensively for Puerto Rican sovereignty.

The Young Patriots was a group of disillusioned whites who felt they were powerless and thus organized to address high unemployment rates and income inequality in Chicago. They organized to get poor whites to challenge systems of inequality and urged them to do so by working together with communities of color. Most of these poor whites had moved north after World War II. Many people referred to the part of town they lived in as "Hillbilly Harlem."[5] The group was revolutionary because they challenged the lack of resources that poor whites had access to without throwing Blacks under the bus or scapegoating communities of color. They recognized that their struggles were connected.[6]

The Fight for LGBTQ Rights

Marsha P. Johnson was a Black trans woman who was at the frontlines of the Stonewall Riots, a series of violent clashes between the LGBTQ community and police. The riots began when the police raided the Stonewall Inn, a gay bar, in New York City. This was in 1969, when being gay was illegal. Johnson was one of the most prominent gay rights activists of the time. Throughout her life, she pushed for the gay rights movement to be more intersectional and address the needs of its most marginalized communities.

All three organizations could have organized for change independently but understood the value and importance of intersectionality. They recognized the ways in which race, class, and gender impacted their lives differently and were able to connect these differences to the same source.

Water Is Life: The #NoDAPL Protests

In 2016, protests erupted across North Dakota in response to the approved construction of Energy Transfer Partners' Dakota Access Pipeline. It was a pipeline expected to span from North Dakota to Illinois, and under a body of water that was near the Standing Rock Indian Reservation. Those who protested the pipeline did so on the grounds that it was disrespectful to ancient tribal burial grounds, and in the event of the pipeline bursting, it would jeopardize the clean drinking water. The protests began when in April 2016, LaDonna Brave Bull established an encampment that she hoped would be a site of cultural preservation to the Indigenous people of the area. The camp grew to thousands of people, and supporters came from near and far to stand against the pipeline. As the number of people standing against the pipeline grew, so did the police and National Guard's response, which included attack dogs, armed soldiers, police in riot gear, and military equipment.

Although it was inspiring to see the momentum the protests were able to sustain, what was most inspiring was the intersectional nature of the protests. Spearheaded by women, the voices of women were front and center in the movement. Tokata Iron Eyes, a 12-year-old Lakota youth

LaDonna Brave Bull asks the Army Corps of Engineers to block the proposed pipeline.

organizer, had this to say in an interview about the protests:

"The role of Indigenous young women coming together in this campaign has also been paramount, signaling the enduring strength of Indigenous women's leadership in questions of tribal governance. Women were the people who held the tribe together and they were the willpower of the tribe and its strength. So, just knowing that we come from such powerful genes makes us feel strong inside."[7]

The #NoDAPL protest, as it came to be called, was a true example of intersectionality. On the surface, the Dakota Access Pipeline was about environmental concerns. But what the movement made clear was the deep connection between environmental justice, racism, and social class. The movement highlighted that it was poor communities of color who are most impacted by environmental devastation. What many people did not realize was that the pipeline was initially supposed to be built through the neighborhoods of white middle-class communities. These communities objected to the pipeline's placement for the same reason that Indigenous protestors and their allies would later voice.[8] However, because of race and social class, their white middle-class voices carried more weight, and the planned pipeline was rerouted to pass through sacred Native burial sites and near the Standing Rock reservation. Any spill from the oil pipeline would contaminate the entirety of the reservation's water supply. The Dakota Access Pipeline protests were an intersectional struggle that brought people together across lines of race, gender, and class. No one had to wonder whether it was an economic, racial, or gender justice issue because it clearly was all three at the same time.

CHAPTER 6

Practicing Solidarity

Now that we know what intersectionality means, what do we do with that knowledge? It is not enough to see and understand our experiences through an intersectional lens. We must begin to live our lives in a way that honors those differences and fights to end all forms of racial, class, and gender oppression. How do we do this? Stand in solidarity with one another. What is solidarity? It is the ties in society that bind people together. Solidarity is a kind of unity that exists between members of an oppressed group and their allies. Solidarity does not occur naturally; it is something we must learn how to do. It is like a muscle: The more we exercise it, the better we will be at doing it.

In 1971, Lila Watson, an Aboriginal woman and activist who was working on anti-Apartheid campaigns, said this: "If you have come to help me, you are wasting your time. If you have come because your

Students from multiple schools gather during a March for Our Lives rally at the University of Georgia.

liberation is bound up with mine, then let us work together."[1] Watson made it clear that solidarity was not charity or an act of pity. It was a duty and one that was performed to the mutual benefit of all involved. An understanding of intersectionality should spark a sense of solidarity in each of us, but much like the former, the latter is a word that has become very popular in recent years. But what exactly does it mean, and how do we put it in practice?

Basics of Being an Ally

No two people share the same experiences or identity, which means that no two people experience oppression in the exact same way. How can we show support for people whose experiences do not mirror our own? How can we stand in solidarity with people who come from different walks of life than we do? This is called being an ally. Being an ally means standing in support of people who may not be part of your own community. It is especially important for people in dominant groups to be allies to marginalized groups. Those with more political and economic power must leverage their privilege to benefit those in society who have less. To be a good ally, one must do three things: listen and learn, commit, and pass the mic.

Listen and Learn

What does allyship look like? While it depends on the context and situation, everyone is capable of being an ally. There are certain things that all good allies have in common. Good allies are able to understand and accept their role in perpetuating systems of oppression against other people. For example, men can be effective allies to women once they realize that they benefit from a system that harms women and then begin working to change this. White people can be effective allies to people of color once they realize that they benefit from a system that harms people of color and then begin working to change this. Effective allyship means realizing that systems of oppression hurt everyone, even those with more privilege, and the only way for everyone to live full and meaningful lives is to change these systems.

Commit to Change

An effective ally realizes that allyship is not a costume that can be shed and then put back on when it is convenient. Just as oppressed communities cannot take off their identities, good allies know that standing with marginalized communities is not a onetime event but a lifelong commitment.

Two friends listen and learn from each other over coffee.

Pass the Mic

The most important thing that good allies do is amplify the voices of people who directly experience trauma due to their identity. Good allies pass the mic. They use their own voices to speak alongside marginalized ones, instead of attempting to speak for them.

It is only when we learn to be good allies to each other that we can truly learn to be in solidarity. Solidarity is hard work. Luckily, the world is full of examples of solidarity in action.

We should listen to people's lived experiences and take our cue from those most directly impacted by oppression.

Solidarity Beyond Borders: Black4Palestine

In the summer of 2014, protests erupted across the United States in response to the police killing of an unarmed Black teenager named Michael Brown. He was shot six times. His body was left in the middle of the street for four hours before it was removed. As protests and riots erupted across Ferguson, Missouri, where Brown had been killed, protestors were met with violent police suppression. The National Guard was deployed, and protestors were routinely attacked with sound grenades and tear gas.

Far across the world, Palestinians living under Israeli occupation were no strangers to racism and police repression. Palestinian activists took to the internet and began posting pictures of support, and instructions on how to treat the inhalation of tear gas and wounds caused by rubber bullets.[2] What could Black Americans and Palestinians have in common when they didn't even share a language? What they *did* share was solidarity. This inspired the Black-Palestinian Solidarity campaign, launched by prominent Black and Palestinian activists all over the world to highlight the shared experiences of both

African Americans in New York rally in support of Palestinian human rights.

communities with police brutality and racism. They said their purpose was to "build with one another in a shoulder to shoulder struggle."[3] This is what true solidarity requires us to do. It asks us to see all people as worthy of justice and dignity, and then work our hardest to create a world where this is a possibility. What the campaign was able to articulate was that a world where Blacks were free could not be possible in world where Palestinians were not also liberated. No one is free until everyone is free.

Solidarity Between Students

Now that we've looked at an example of solidarity around the world, what does solidarity look like closer to home? What does solidarity look like in schools? How can students commit to being better allies to one another?

Many schools have affinity groups that are based on certain identities, like Black student unions, Latinx student unions, gay-straight alliances, and others. One way to show support for marginalized students is by attending one of these club meetings and asking how you can support the work they are doing at school.

Being an ally also looks like being a good friend. Solidarity means interrupting oppression when you see it happening at school. For example, if a classmate calls someone a racial slur, a good ally will interrupt this kind of behavior. Interrupting oppression is not easy. It takes courage. But to change the world, we must be willing to step outside our comfort zones and take risks.

The Parkland Survivors and New Gun Control Campaigns

In response to the devastating school shooting in Parkland, Florida, that killed 17 people, a student movement emerged across the country. Led by the students who survived the attack in Florida, the movement quickly gained momentum as students from all communities and walks of life joined the conversation. Many of the young student leaders recognized the need for an intersectional analysis of gun violence. Parkland survivors met with students from Chicago in an attempt to combat gun violence nationwide. Emma Gonzalez, one of the survivors of the Parkland massacre, had this to say: "People of color in inner-cities have been dealing with this for a despicably long time."[4]

The Parkland survivors have turned their collective trauma into a movement for national change.

History has shown us that it has never been individuals who have changed the world on their own. The world has only ever been changed for the better by the masses of people standing in solidarity with one another. A better world is possible. We just have to work together to achieve it.

Chapter Notes

Chapter 1
Identity and Intersectionality

1. "Introducing Ernest Hemingway," LSJ.com, https://www.lsj.org/web/literature/hemingway.php (accessed March 2018).
2. Kimberlé Crenshaw, "Mapping the Margins: Intersectionality, Identity Politics, and Violence against Women of Color," *Stanford Law Review* 43, no. 6 (1991).
3. Bim Adewunmi, "Kimberlé Crenshaw on Intersectionality," *New Statesman*, April 20, 2018, https://www.newstatesman.com/lifestyle/2014/04/kimberl-crenshaw-intersectionality-i-wanted-come-everyday-metaphor-anyone-could.
4. Audre Lorde, "Learning from the 60s," *Sister Outsider: Essays and Speeches by Audre Lorde* (Berkeley, CA: Crossing Press, 2007), p. 138.
5. Ibid.
6. Audre Lorde, *"The Cancer Journals"* (San Francisco, CA: Aunt Lute Books, 1997).
7. Audre Lorde, "There is No Hierarchy of Oppression," *I am Your Sister: Collected and Unpublished Writings of Audre Lorde* (Oxford, England: Oxford University Press, 2011), p. 219.

Chapter 2
Understanding Race

1. "Bacon's Rebellion," NPS.gov, https://www.nps.gov/jame/learn/historyculture/bacons-rebellion.htm (accessed March 2018).
2. "Women's Rights and the Antislavery Connection," NPS.gov, https://www.nps.gov/wori/learn/historyculture/antislavery-connection.htm (accessed March 2018).

3. Elaine Brown, *A Taste of Power: A Black Woman's Story* (New York, NY: Pantheon Books, 1992), p. 367.

Chapter 3
Understanding Gender

1. Cheris Kramarae, Paula A. Treichler, and Ann Russo, *A Feminist Dictionary*, (Ontario, Canada: Pandora Press, 1985).
2. "Unity Principles," Womensmarch.com, https://www.womensmarch.com/mission (accessed March 2018).
3. "How Racism Tainted Women's Suffrage," NPR.org, https://www.npr.org/2011/03/25/134849480/the-root-how-racism-tainted-womens-suffrage (accessed March 2018).
4. Ta-Nehisi Coates, "Frederick Douglass: A Women's Rights Man," *Atlantic*, September 20, 2011, https://www.theatlantic.com/personal/archive/2011/09/frederick-douglass-a-womens-rights-man/245977.
5. "Seneca Falls Convention," History.com, https://www.history.com/this-day-in-history/seneca-falls-convention-begins (accessed March 2018).
6. Sojourner Truth, "Aint I a Woman?" (speech, Akron, Ohio, 1851), National Park Service, https://www.nps.gov/articles/sojourner-truth.htm.
7. Ibid.
8. "Betty Friedan," NWHM.org, https://www.nwhm.org/education-resources/biographies/betty-friedan (accessed March 2018).
9. Stephanie Coontz, "Friedan Exposed 1950s Women's Emotional Core," *Women's eNews*, June 10, 2011, https://womensenews.org/2011/06/friedan-exposed-1950s-womens-emotional-core.

10. bell hooks, *Ain't I a Woman: Black Women and Feminism* (Boston, MA: South End Press, 1981).

Chapter 4

Understanding Class

1. Megan Leonhardt, "The Lasting Effects of Occupy Wall Street," *Time*, September 16, 2016, http://time.com/money/4495707/occupy-wall-street-anniversary-effects.
2. Christopher Ingraham, "The Richest 1% Owns More of the Country's Wealth than at Any Time in the Past 50 Years," *Washington Post,* December 6, 2017, https://www.washingtonpost.com/news/wonk/wp/2017/12/06/the-richest-1-percent-now-owns-more-of-the-countrys-wealth-than-at-any-time-in-the-past-50-years/?utm_term=.87ba26c07858.
3. Christopher Ingraham, "American Land Barons," *Washington Post*, December 21, 2017, https://www.washingtonpost.com/news/wonk/wp/2017/12/21/american-land-barons-100-wealthy-families-now-own-nearly-as-much-land-as-that-of-new-england/?utm_term=.f8ecae5ecd9a.
4. "America's Shrinking Middle Class," PewSocialTrends.org, http://www.pewsocialtrends.org/2016/05/11/americas-shrinking-middle-class-a-close-look-at-changes-within-metropolitan-areas (accessed March 2018).
5. Dennis Gilbert, *The American Class Structure in an Age of Growing Inequality.* 4th ed. (Belmont: Wadsworth Company, Year), pp. 235–236.

6. "What is the Current Poverty Rate in the United States?" UCDavis.edu, https://poverty.ucdavis.edu/faq/what-current-poverty-rate-united-states (accessed March 2018).

7. Ethan Earle, "A Brief History of Occupy Wall Street," Rosa Luxemburg Stiftung, November 2012, http://www.rosalux-nyc.org/a-history-of-occupy.

8. Ezra Klein, "Who are the 99 Percent?" *Washington Post,* October 4, 2011, https://www.washingtonpost.com/blogs/ezra-klein/post/who-are-the-99-percent/2011/08/25/gIQAt87jKL_blog.html?utm_term=.7704ec37a454.

9. Angela Davis, "The 99%: A Community of Resistance," *Guardian*, November 15, 2011, https://www.theguardian.com/commentisfree/cifamerica/2011/nov/15/99-percent-community-resistance.

Chapter 5

Many Struggles, One Movement

1. Shannon Ridgway, "Oppression Olympics: The Games We Shouldn't Be Playing," *Everyday Feminism,* November 4, 2012, https://everydayfeminism.com/2012/11/oppression-olympics.

2. Audre Lorde, "There is No Hierarchy of Oppression," *I am Your Sister: Collected and Unpublished Writings of Audre Lorde* (Oxford, England: Oxford University Press, 2011), p. 219.

3. "The Original Rainbow Coalition: Multi-Racial Poor People's Organizing in Chicago and Beyond," Kairoscenter.org, https://kairoscenter.org/original-rainbow-coalition-seminar.

4. "Police Kill Two Members of the Black Panther Party," History.com, https://www.history.com/this-day-in-history/police-kill-two-members-of-the-black-panther-party (accessed March 2018).

5. Michael Mccanne, "The Panthers and the Patriots," *Jacobin*, May 19, 2017, https://www.jacobinmag.com/2017/05/black-panthers-young-patriots-fred-hampton.
6. Ibid.
7. Jaskiran Dhillon, "Indigenous Youth are Building a Climate Justice Movement by Targeting Colonialism," Truthout, June 20, 2016, http://www.truth-out.org/news/item/36482-indigenous-youth-are-building-a-climate-justice-movement-by-targeting-colonialism.
8. T.J. Raphael, "Bismarck Residents got the Dakota Access Pipeline Moved Without a Fight," PRI, December 01, 2016, https://www.pri.org/stories/2016-12-01/bismarck-residents-got-dakota-access-pipeline-moved-without-fight.

Chapter 6
Practicing Solidarity

1. "Voice of the Day: Lila Watson," SOJO.net, https://sojo.net/articles/voice-day-lilla-watson (accessed March 2018).
2. Robert Mackey, "Advice for Ferguson's Protestors from the Middle East," *New York Times,* August 14, 2014, https://www.nytimes.com/2014/08/15/world/middleeast/advice-for-fergusons-protesters-from-the-middle-east.html.
3. "When I See Them, I See Us," Black Palestinian Solidarity Network, http://www.blackpalestiniansolidarity.com/about.html.
4. P.R. Lockhard, "Students from Parkland and Chicago unite to Expand the Gun Control Conversation," *Vox*, March 6, 2018, https://www.vox.com/identities/2018/3/6/17086426/parkland-chicago-students-gun-violence-race-activism.

Glossary

abolition The action of ending a system, practice, or institution.

ally Someone who is supportive of and advocates for marginalized groups.

ethnicity The fact or state of belonging to a social group that has a common national or cultural identity.

feminism The advocacy of women's rights on the basis of the equality of the sexes.

hierarchy A system in which people or groups are above or below the other according to status.

identity The distinguishing character or personality of an individual.

Indigenous Originating or being native to a particular place.

intersectionality The interconnected nature of social categorizations such as race, class, and gender as they apply to a given individual or group.

oppression A situation in which people are governed in an unfair and cruel way and prevented from having opportunities and freedom.

organizing The coordination of cooperative efforts to promote the welfare of a community.

race A category of people who share certain inherited physical characteristics, such as skin color and facial features. Race is a social construct.

social class A division of society based on social and economic status.

solidarity Unity and mutual support among individuals or groups with a common interest.

Further Reading

Books

Adiche, Chimamanda. *We Should All be Feminists*. London, England: 4th Estate Press, 2014.

Alexander, Michelle. *The New Jim Crow: Mass Incarceration in the Age of Colorblindness*. New York, NY: The New Press, 2010.

Desmond, Matthew. *Evicted: Poverty and Profit in the American City*. New York, NY: Crown Books, 2016.

Ehrenreich, Barbara. *Nickle and Dimed: On Not Getting by in America*. New York, NY: Henry Holt and Co., 2001.

Websites

Black Lives Matter
BlackLivesMatter.com
The Black Lives Matter official website has a timeline of the movement from emergence to present, regularly posts updates on the movement, and links to current campaigns and ways to participate.

Do Something
DoSomething.org
Do Something is a global movement for good. It mobilizes young people across the world by helping them connect to social justice projects and campaigns that are happening around them.

Everyday Feminism
EverydayFeminism.com

Everyday Feminism is an accessible educational platform that hopes to help people understand systems of power and oppression so that they may challenge them in their own lives.

Showing Up for Racial Justice
ShowingUpForRacialJustice.org

SURJ is a grassroots national organization that is building a multiracial movement to end white supremacy and create a racially just society.

Index